Dedication

I would like to dedicate this book
to my Teachers:

Ms. Henderson (My Grade2 Teacher)

Ms. Suter (My Grade1 Teacher)

Ms. Vella and Ms. Ross (My SK Teachers)

Ms. Lucyk and Ms. Cornacchia (My JK Teachers)

Thank you for teaching me how to read.

This Book Belongs to

_____

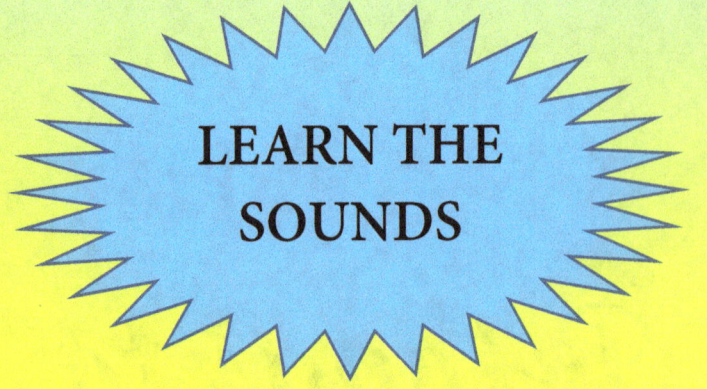

LEARN THE SOUNDS

DANCE MOVES

Author and Illustrator: Arushi Bhattacharjee

Editor: Robin Katz

Illustrators of Bonus Stories:

Avneet Kaur Dhaliwal & Navena Thelepan

Special thanks to our Kickstarter Supporters who have helped bring this book to life.

A shout out to our Kickstarter Winners

Kinnari, Andrea, Scott and Isaac

THE CAT AND THE RAT

The **cat** has a **bat**.

The **rat** has a **hat**.

The **cat** plays with the **rat**.

The **cat** and the **rat** sit on a **mat**.

TRACE THE WORDS

cat cat

rat rat

bat bat

hat hat

mat mat

LET'S GET WET

This is Jet.

Jet is my **pet**.

Jet gets me **wet**.

We are all **wet**.

WORD SEARCH

_et Word Family

Find words that end in *et*

a	l	e	t	d	i	m
b	f	c	w	e	g	e
v	q	g	e	t	h	t
e	j	e	t	r	j	a
t	o	m	u	s	k	l
w	p	n	p	e	t	c
z	x	b	e	t	m	o
n	e	t	r	p	u	i

THE PIG LIKES TO DIG

The **pig** digs up a **fig**.

The **fig** is **big**.

The **pig** does a **jig**.

The **pig** eats the **fig**.

MAZE

_ig Word Family

Color the words that end in _ig

pig	fig	go	tea	dip
ball	big	car	boy	sea
me	dig	jig	wig	tall
egg	jug	elf	zig	rat
can	do	my	rig	gig

BOP TO THE POP!

Let us **bop** to this **pop**!

The girls sing and **hop**.

The boys play and **bop**.

Bop! **Bop**! Dance to the **pop**!

MATCH

_op Word Family

Match the words to the picture

TOP

BOP

MOP

BONUS
DANCE MOVES

FUN IN THE SUN

The girl has a **bun**.

She likes to **run**.

We play in the **sun**.

We all have **fun**.

RHYMING WORDS

Write a word that ends in *un* (Use Picture Clues)

I see the _ _ _

I like to eat a _ _ _

I can _ _ _

...By Avneet

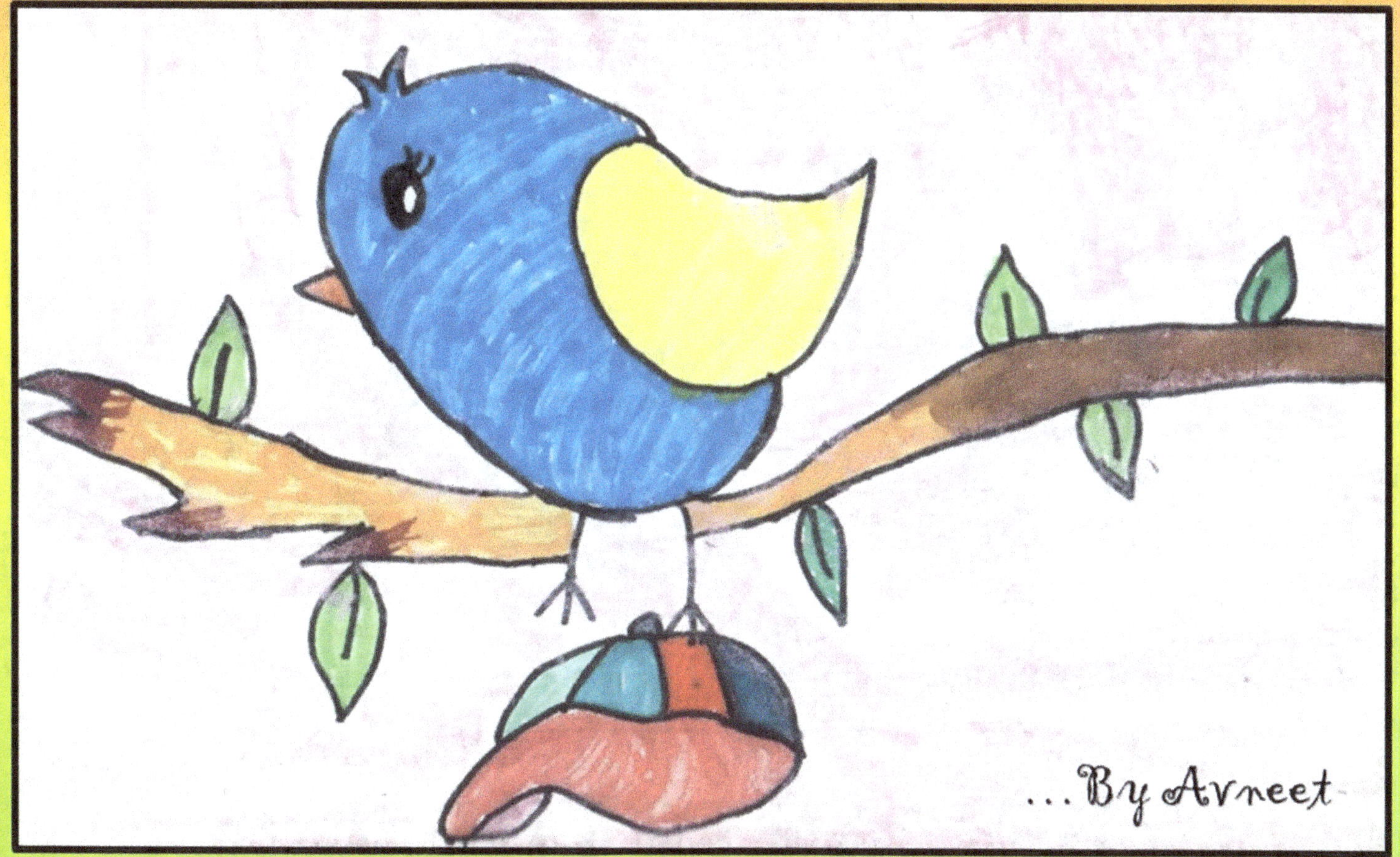

ZAP AND HIS CAP

Zap has a **cap**.
Zap takes a **nap**.
A bird flies away with his **cap**.
The **cap** falls on his **lap**.

...By Navena

THE MAN IN THE VAN

The **man** drives a **van**.
He puts a **can** in the **van**.
The **man** slips on the **can**.
Then he rests under the **fan**.

About the Author

Arushi is a seven-year-old student in Grade 2 at Seneca Trail Public School in Ontario, Canada. She was born in Texas and later moved to Toronto with her family.

Canadian winters bring some of Arushi's favorite adventures: Decorating Christmas trees, building snowmen, and going tobogganing with her sister. Arushi also loves taking ballet lessons and has become a great fan of dance and music!

For creating this book, Arushi was inspired by her older sister, Anushka, a child author herself. Both girls are avid readers, so it's no surprise that they're so excited about writing books!

It was Arushi's goal to write an educational book to help children start their reading journey. She completed the manuscript and illustrations as a project during her winter break.

Arushi and Anushka are very active in their community. The author sisters donate part of their proceeds to charitable organizations like the Durham Children's Aid Association.

Arushi hopes kids will enjoy reading and completing the activities in this book as much as she has enjoyed creating them!

Connect with Arushi on Social Media

SOCIAL MEDIA LINK

1. Open your Phone Camera
2. Scan this QR
3. Click on the Link that pops up

https://www.instagram.com/ArushiAnushkaChildAuthors

https://www.facebook.com/ArushiAnushkaChildAuthors

About the Illustrators of Bonus Stories

Arushi collaborated with her classmates Avneet and Navena to work on the bonus stories!

Navena Thelepan is a seven-year-old student in Grade 2 at Seneca Trail Public School. Her hobbies are drawing, painting and making crafts. She also does extra-curricular activities like playing tennis, swimming, music and piano. Navena is a Black Belt in karate (Tae Kwon Do).

Avneet Kaur Dhaliwal studies in Grade 2 at Seneca Trail Public School. Her hobbies are reading, drawing and painting. She loves skating and ballet.

CHILD AUTHORS

Published at Age 6 and 8

Educational Books

Story Books

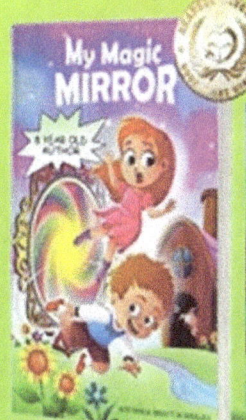

Activity Books

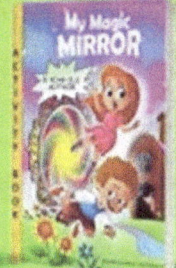

amazon

Indigo

BARNES & NOBLE

www.ingramcontent.com/pod-product-compliance
Lightning Source LLC
Chambersburg PA
CBHW081013120626
46546CB00010B/3130